I0800043

WonderWorks

Decodable Reader

Unit 10

McGraw Hill

Contents

Cole Woke Up
by Helen Reading
illustrated by Eva Vagreti
1

Life at a Dune
by Jorge Garcia
9

Queen Bee Dee
by Nyasha King
illustrated by Pat Lucas-Morris
17

Cole Woke Up

by Helen Reading
illustrated by Eva Vagreti

Where is Cole?
Cole is in bed at home.
Cole can doze.

The sun came up.
Did Cole wake up?
No, Cole did not get up.

Mom came in.
The sun did not wake Cole.
Can Mom get Cole up?

"**Look** at the time.
It is time to wake up.
It is time to go."

Cole did not get up.
Mom sat on the bed.
"Cole, it is not a joke.
You can not get up late."

Mom woke Cole.

Look at Cole wake up!

It is time for Cole to go!

Life at a Dune

by Jorge Garcia

Danita Delimont/Gallo Images/Getty Images

Manuel Gutjahr/Vetta/Getty Images

Take a look at a dune.
It can make a **good** home.
Who can make a home
here?

Juniors Bildarchiv/Alamy

Is it cute?
It can hop, hop, hop.
It can dig a big hole. The dune is quite hot on top.

It can dig, dig, dig.
It can use a safe home.
It can hide in a dune.

Manuel Gutjahr/Vetta/Getty Images

It can ride up, up, up.
It can sit on top.
It can dip and dive.
It can zig zag.

Danita Delimont/Gallo Images/Getty Images

It can hide in a dune.
It can gaze side to side.
Can it gaze up?

Tim McCabe, USDA Natural Resources Conservation Service

We can make a rule to save a dune.
It can make a fine home!

Queen Bee Dee

by Nyasha King
illustrated by Pat Lucas-Morris

Dee can tug at a bee sock.
Dee has bee feet.
Dee can be a big bee.

Dee is not quite a bee yet.
Mom gave Dee a tan bag.
What can be in this bag?

Dee can peek in the sack.

Does Dee need it?

Yes!

Mom can set it on Dee.

Mom set it on top.

Does Dee seem like a bee?

Yes!

Come, see the big bee!
It can not be Dee.
It is a queen bee!

Dee gave Mom a big hug.
Meet Dee, the queen bee!

Unit 10

Word Count: 94

Decodable Words

Target Phonics Element: Long *o* (*o_e, o*)
Cole, doze, go, home, joke, no, woke
Review: *at, bed, came, can, did, get, in, it, late, Mom, not, on, sat, sun, time, up, wake*

High-Frequency Words

look, where
Review: *a, for, is, the, to, you*

Word Count: 110

Decodable Words

Target Phonics Element: Long *u* (*u_e*)
cute, dune, rule, use
Review: *at, big, but, can, dig, dip, dive, fine, gaze, hide, hole, home, hop, hot, in, it, kick, life, make, not, on, pick, quite, safe, save, side, sit, ride, take, top, up, yes, zag, zig*

High-Frequency Words

good, who
Review: *a, and, do, here, is, look, to*

Week 3 • *Queen Bee Dee* .... page 17

Word Count: 98

Decodable Words

Target Phonics Element: Long *e* (*ee, e*)
be, bee, Dee, feet, meet, need, peek, queen, see, seem
Review: *at, bag, big, can, cute, gave, hug, in, it, Mom, not, on, quite, sack, set, sock, top, tug, yet*

High-Frequency Words

come, does
Review: *a, and, has, help, is, like, she, the, this, what*

Decoding skills taught to date:

Consonants /m/*m*, /s/*s*, /p/*p*, /t/*t*; Short *a*; Short *i*; Initial and Final /n/*n*; Initial /k/*c*; Short *o*; Initial and Final /d/*d*; Consonant /h/*h*; Short *e*; Blends *sn, sp, st*; Consonants /f/*f*, /r/*r*; Initial and Final /b/*b*; Consonant /l/*l*; Initial /k/*k*; Digraph *ck*; Short *u*; Initial and Final /g/*g*; Consonant /w/*w*; Consonants /ks/*x*, /v/*v*; Consonants /j/*j*, /qu/*qu*; Consonants /y/*y*, /z/*z*; Long *a* (*a_e*); Long *i* (*i_e*); Long *o* (*o_e, o*); Long *u* (*u_e*); Long *e* (*e_e, ee, e*)